Joseph Chalmers, O.Carm.
Prior General

In Allegiance to Jesus Christ

Joseph Chalmers, O.Carm.
Prior General

In Allegiance to Jesus Christ

Ten conferences on Carmelite Life

Edizioni Carmelitane

Roma

Cover photo by Fr. William Harry O.Carm.

First Printing: 1999
Second Printing: 2004

ISBN 88-7288-051-3

© Edizioni Carmelitane
Via Sforza Pallavicini, 10
00193 Roma - Italia

Finito di stampare nel settembre 2004
dalla Tipografia Città Nuova della P.A.M.O.M.
via San Romano in Garfagnana, 23 - 00148 Roma
Telefono & fax 06.65.30.467
e-mail: segr.tipografia@cittanuova.it

CURIA GENERALIZIA DEI CARMELITANI
00184 ROMA (ITALIA) - VIA GIOVANNI LANZA, 138
E-MAIL seggen @ocarm.org
TEL. 06462 018 1 FAX 06462 018 47

4th April 1999
Easter Sunday

Dear Fellow Carmelite,

The General Council asked me to make available to a wider audience some of the talks which I have given during the three years since the General Chapter 1995. This book is the result of that request.

The individual chapters began life as talks given at Provincial Chapters or Regional meetings or other gatherings of the Carmelite Family. I have edited them for publication but no doubt there exists some overlapping of themes because they all focus on our Carmelite tradition.

I hope that whoever reads this book may gain some fruit from it. I shall be very happy if, in some way, it increases our commitment to what God desires to do within us so that we may come to see all that happens as if with the eyes of God (Cf. Const. 78) and to love as God loves.

Sincerely,

Joseph Chalmers O. Carm.

Joseph Chalmers, O. Carm.
Prior General

INDEX

CARMEL: A PLACE AND A JOURNEY INTO THE THIRD MILLENNIUM

The General Chapter of 1995 was the last to be held this century and it launched the Carmelite Order towards the new millennium. At the Chapter we tackled three principal tasks:- 1) To examine and approve new Constitutions; 2) To elect a Prior General and General Council and 3) To examine the theme, "Carmel: A Place and a Journey into the Third Millennium – Our Mission Today – 'Get up and eat lest the journey be too long' (1 Kg. 19,7).

For many years and at many international meetings the Order has focused on our Carmelite identity. It was felt now to be time to reflect on Carmel's mission. The "place" mentioned in the theme is for us of course Mount Carmel which stands for the fundamental values of our Carmelite life. These values are well expressed in the new Constitutions.

The concept of journey speaks to us of a dynamic reality. We are on the way but to where? Towards the third millennium certainly – towards the future but what will the future hold for us? We are invited into God's future who alone knows what that will be and who is already constructing the future out of our present. We are laying the foundations now for what we will be in the future.

We are told in the new Constitutions (art. 14) that Carmelites follow Christ above all by committing ourselves to searching for the face of the Living God (the contemplative dimension of life), to community and to service in the midst of the people. These values are intimately related to one another. They are united by means of the experience of the desert. Carmelites are committed to make of Christ crucified, naked and emptied, the foundation of our lives. We are to destroy every obstacle which prevents us from being perfectly dependent on him and every obstacle which prevents us loving God and others perfectly. The process of stripping away everything that is

not God, which leads to union with God, is called in our spiritual tradition "puritas cordis" and "vacare Deo", concepts which express
total openness to God and a progressive self-emptying.

When, through this process we arrive at the point where we can
see the whole of reality with the eyes of God, our attitude towards
the world will be transformed and this changed view will be incarnat-
ed in our life of community and service. The two figures who
inspire us above all to follow Christ in this way are of course the
Prophet Elijah and Our Lady, the Mother of Carmel.

The Call to be Contemplative

The Carmelite is called to be a contemplative. Contemplatives do
not only live in enclosed monasteries. There are many contemplatives who live in the midst of a very busy world. There are contemplatives in every neighbourhood and in every area of life. The word
"contemplative" does not refer to a state but a way of relating to
God. By our Carmelite vocation, we are called to be contemplatives
but what does that mean in practice?

What does it mean to seek the face of the Living God? Surely we
have been taught from our earliest years that God is everywhere and
therefore does not need to be sought? However it is also true that
God is very elusive. God cannot be grasped by the human mind. We
know by experience that God alone can ultimately satisfy us since we
have been created with a capacity for God. God's desire is to unite
with us in a way which is beyond the power of human words to
describe. This is God's gift but it will not be given to anyone who
does not wish to receive it. I think that what God wants to give us is
beautifully summed up in the following reading from the letter to the
Ephesians:

> This then is what I pray, kneeling before the Father from whom every
> family whether spiritual or natural takes its name, that out of His infinite
> glory He may grant you the power, through His Spirit, for your hidden
> self to grow strong so that Christ may live in your hearts through faith
> and then planted in love and built on love, you will with all the saints
> have strength to grasp the breadth and the length, the height and the
> depth; until knowing the love of Christ which is beyond all knowledge,
> you are filled with the utter fullness of God. Glory be to Him who
> wants to do far more for us than we could ask for or even imagine.

Glory be to Him in the Church and in Christ Jesus for ever and ever. Amen (Eph. 3, 14-21).

The writer wants us to be filled with the utter fullness of God. To be filled with the utter fullness of God is to be a mystic. Mysticism or contemplation is not for an elite few: it is for everyone. Remember the prophetic words of Karl Rahner, "The Christian of the future will be a mystic or will not be a Christian at all." To be a mystic means to become an intimate friend of God. This is the call which we receive in baptism and mysticism or contemplation is the full flowering of the baptismal grace. In our world we are witnessing a thirst for prayer, a thirst for God. Carmelite spirituality can lead people to the source of living water where their thirst can be quenched. As Carmelites we are not only expected to be good parish priests or teachers but also and above all we are expected to be able to lead people in their search for God. We are expected to speak of God from our own experience.

In order to be able to lead people to the Source of living water, we must know something of the desert which is a necessary and integral part of our vocation. The desert can take many forms. It may come in the form of an illness or an appointment to some difficult position or the failure to be elected to a position of authority, or removal from some apostolate which we have made our own, or from a community where we have become very comfortable and so on. God uses the ordinary things of life to challenge us to grow, to move from where we are to where we can be. This is a difficult journey which we really do not want to make and so God gives us a push to get us moving and to continue our journey when we get stuck.

The desert is where God erupts into our comfortable little world and knocks down some of the things which have provided our security in the past so that we might learn by experience that our security can only be based in God. The desert never comes in a way that we expect so that we cannot control what is happening.

The faith to which we are called is very radical since it goes to the roots of our existence as we are gradually transformed to become what God knows we can be. We are asked to take the risk of letting go control of our own lives and allowing God to take control. Mary, our Mother and our sister, points the way for us. She allowed God to have full freedom in her life and she challenges us to do the same. Too often we make Our Lady into a plaster cast statue and say lovely prayers to her but we ignore what she says to us through the pages of Scripture. Remember what she said to the servants at the wedding feast – "Do whatever he tells you". (Jn. 2,5)

Called to form community

We seek God alone not as isolated individuals but as a community which needs to be continually built up because it does not grow naturally. We have been called to live as members of a community. Living fully this very important element of our vocation is prophetic in that it points out that the love of Christ can break down the walls of division which human beings use to separate themselves from others. Community is God's gift to us because relationships are essential to our growth. We can all be very good at loving our neighbour if we never have to meet him or her. Community living can at times be difficult but it is through close interaction with other human beings that we grow.

We are unique individuals but we share a common heritage. We seek the face of God together and we find God in and through one another. Community is an important element of our way to God. Our love for God is proved by the way we treat one another. Do you love God? If you really want to know the answer to that question, just ask the members of your community.

The value of building community is very much connected with the first value of being a contemplative because how we relate to other people depends very much on how we relate to God. If we can begin to look on creation and see things as God sees them, then our relationships with others will bring them life and freedom. Until God has purified us, our tendency is to manipulate people, very subtly at times, to conform to what we desire. Love must be unconditional or it is a form of manipulation. God's way of loving is unconditional ; our way is conditional on the response we get. So our way of loving must be purified and the only way this can happen is if God does it. God respects us totally and will only accomplish this if we co-operate.

We need to consent daily to the presence and action of God in our lives, remembering always that God's ways are not our ways. God will act in our lives to purify us in ways that may seem very strange to us. If we are to recognise the presence and action of God at work in our lives we must tune into God's wavelength. The only way of doing that is by spending time, quality time, alone with God and seeking God together with the members of our community.

Called to serve

The third fundamental Carmelite value is to serve in the midst of people. We know that the Carmelites at a very early stage changed their lifestyle from hermits to mendicant friars. The fundamental idea of the mendicant movement was to provide a different model of following Christ than that of the monks. The mendicant ideal was to find God at the heart of the world and to serve people where they were.

We know that what makes the Carmelite is not the particular work but the underlying attitudes with which the work is approached. If we truly have tasted God in our prayer, we will want to share this love with the people whom we are called to serve. We know that love cannot be just words but must be very practical.

The choice which the early Carmelites made to become mendicant friars has deeply marked Carmelite spirituality. The desert and the mountain top, where one can be alone with God, still exercise a fascination for the Carmelite. There is a need to find space where one can be alone with God but the desert is often to be found among people.

St. John of the Cross once said that a single drop of divine love is worth far more than all the good works. This means that much more is accomplished through a life which is totally surrendered to God than by many good works which are vitiated by egoism. When our lives are totally surrendered to God, we are like God and we love as God loves. Therefore our very being brings life to others. The work of surrendering our lives to God totally is truly the work of a life time and is the hardest work we will ever do.

Our prayer, our work and our community lives are to form a seamless whole. Our prayer will make us more involved in the service of our neighbour because the point of prayer is not to feel good but to see with the eyes of God and to love with the heart of God. In turn our apostolic work will force us back to prayer as we see that we can do nothing without God but that with God all things are possible. Our community life is a fruitful source of our apostolate and is also a proof that the Gospel really works when people see that we can truly live in harmony with one another.

Some Challenges

What then are the challenges which we face as we move into the third millennium? The principal challenge of course is what it has always been – to become what we are called to be. However, among others, I would like to underline the following four concrete challenges:-
1) Vocations and formation
2) The quality of community life
3) A renewal of our commitment to prayer
4) New evangelisation

1. Vocations and Formation

All of us have the serious duty to work and pray for vocations. The best way to attract new vocations is simply to be what we are called to be. The Carmelite ideal has lost none of its attractiveness throughout the centuries. We must of course be where young people are. It is not necessary to be a specialist in this field. Young people are looking for people who will listen to them, without always feeling the need to preach. We do not need to know all the answers. It is essential to have a good policy for vocations ministry and to have communities which will truly be places of welcome for young people who wish to "come and see" (Jn. 1,39) and where they can experience what our life has to offer.

When vocations do come to us, we have the sacred duty to form them according to the Carmelite ideal If we provide an excellent formation for our new vocations this will pay off very well in the years to come. Then whatever sacrifices we have had to make will have been worth it.

Obviously our spirituality is not only for the friars or nuns but is shared by all the groups which make up the Carmelite Family. The charism of an Order is a gift of God for the Church and the world. Therefore an important element of the work for vocations and formation is to share our Carmelite ideals with anyone who is interested. I am thinking here of the many groups which are attached to the Order and also of individuals who are simply attracted by our spirituality. All of these could be said to be members of the Carmelite Family even though the connection might be very loose. In order to share our Carmelite ideals we must not only know them but have interiorised them and live them.

2. The quality of community life

It is very clear that we have been called together as members of a contemplative family and the witness we give is truly prophetic. One of the challenges we have for the future is to work on the quality of our community lives.

We need to examine ourselves individually and as communities. How much time are we willing to give to building up the community? Each of us must ask, "Does my presence add to the happiness of my sisters and brothers or am I a difficulty for them?" It is not enough just to say prayers together or to eat together. Are we willing to talk about and be open about the issues which really matter and which affect the community? People are thirsting for real community. The building up of community requires a lot from us but equally will give us a great deal in return.

3. A Renewal of our commitment to prayer

Prayer is not just words that we say; prayer is our relationship with God. Our vocation is to be transformed – to become a new creation. This is not something we can bring about. It is God's work but it requires of us a total commitment. The way of prayer is very demanding and so there is a great temptation to settle for much less.

By calling for a renewal of commitment to prayer I am not asking for us as individuals or as communities to say more prayers. What I am calling for is a re-commitment to consent to God's presence and action in our lives however that is manifested. Obviously we need to set aside adequate time for personal and community prayer. We need the space and the silence to listen to God who speaks in the depths of our hearts with a still , small voice. If our lives are filled with too much noise, we will not be able to hear this voice. I believe that a renewal in our commitment to prayer will have a profound impact on our personal and community lives and also on our apostolic work.

4. New Evangelisation

We know of the Church's call for an era of new evangelisation as we approach the third millennium. We mentioned in the final document coming from the General Chapter 1995 that we could see in the experience of Elijah an example for ourselves. He was deeply depressed because he believed that, despite his wonderful victory over the prophets of Baal, they had in fact won. He believed that he was alone but God pointed out to Elijah that there were very many who had not bent the knee to Baal. Like Elijah, we are asked to look at our reality with new eyes, to see the good things which are there despite the counter signs. We are to be like the watchers on the towers of the city who are the first to see the dawn. There are signs of light everywhere heralding a new dawn to those with eyes to see.

It is not allowed for a Christian to be a pessimist! We are to be optimists because Christ has already won the victory over sin and death. We are the heralds of Christ. Even when we cannot see any reason for optimism, we are asked to believe in the power of God who is creating even now a new heaven and a new earth.

Perhaps one of the big problems for us in this work of evangelisation is to find a new language to express the unchangeable truths of the faith. Perhaps the traditional language no longer speaks to modern people. In order to find a suitable language it is necessary to soak ourselves in the Gospel message. The best language is a life which has been transformed in God. If we are "filled with the utter fullness of God", we will speak very powerfully to people of the love of. God or rather God will speak very powerfully through us and, using our hands and voices, will touch the hearts of many. Love is not an abstract ideal; it is very practical. If in our apostolic work, we can show people in practice what the love of God is and what it feels like, they are more likely to believe it.

THE FUNDAMENTAL ELEMENTS OF CARMELITE SPIRITUALITY

Throughout the centuries various ways of following Christ have been tried and tested. Some of these ways have endured to our present day and still have the power to attract many people and help them to live a deeper life of allegiance to Jesus Christ. One of these ways is the Carmelite way.

A vocation is a very personal call from God. Each of us has our own particular vocation to become what God knows we can be. An important part of our vocation is our attraction to a particular way of following Christ. Some people are attracted to the Jesuit, or Franciscan or Dominican way but we feel deep within us an attraction to the Carmelite way. No particular spirituality is better than another. They all are intended to help us live the Gospel in the fullest possible way. Our way is the Carmelite way because that is the path to which God has called us.

So what is this Carmelite way? First of all, as with every Christian spirituality, we are called to be followers of Christ. We keep our eyes fixed on him; he is our leader, our teacher, our brother, our saviour, our Lord. We seek to assimilate his message and to live the Gospel in daily life. The Carmelite way of doing this is to commit ourselves to search for the face of the Living God, which is the contemplative dimension of life, to fraternity and to the service of others. These values are intimately related to one another and are united by means of the experience of the desert. Like Elijah, we must pass by way of the desert in order to reach Mount Horeb, the mountain of God. In the desert, the living flame of love burns within us, burning away all that is not God, and preparing us to meet God in the sound of a gentle breeze. We are not alone on this journey. Accompanying us always is Our Lady, our sister and our mother, who gently teaches us how to listen to the still small voice of God and to consent to God's presence and action in our life. Carmel has always been marian and will always be so. We express our devotion to Our Lady in different ways according to our different cultures but all of us seek to live our devotion by becoming like her.

The first hermits on Mount Carmel gathered as a community in order to seek God's will together. Somewhere between 1206 and 1214 these hermits had reached such a unity and common purpose that they decided to make their group more formal by seeking ecclesiastical approval and so they asked Albert, Patriarch of Jerusalem, to write for them a "formula vitae" based on the proposal which they presented to him.

In 1997 we celebrated the 750th anniversary of the definitive approval of the Rule. On this occasion, the Superior General of the Discalced Carmelites and I sent a joint letter to the whole Carmelite Family about the Rule which has been and remains the inspiration for the two Orders. It is not only an historical document but is a real source of inspiration for all Carmelites. The title of our letter was, "Open to God's Future". Our spiritual tradition is not only a great treasure of the past but has the power to inspire us today and in the future.

The Carmelite Rule is brief and we do not possess a copy of the original, written between 1206 and 1214. The oldest version which exists is that definitively approved by Pope Innocent IV in 1247 when the hermits desired to join that new prophetic movement in the Church at the time – the mendicant movement.

There are various ways of reading a text. We can ask what St. Albert meant and what the hermits understood when he wrote. There are also other possible interpretations which go beyond what St. Albert and the hermits actually had in mind. These new interpretations come about by asking the text the questions we have, based on our own experience of life. An ancient text like the Rule can also be studied in a scientific or historical way. All of these different studies and methods of interpretation are important but even more important of course is to live the values contained in the Rule.

It is possible to interpret a text but not allow it to touch us deeply. One can approach a text with the conviction that one already knows very well what it has to say. In this case one runs the risk of not being open to the nuances of the text. The same problem exists when we approach Sacred Scripture. At times familiarity with the words of Jesus can actually be a barrier to what God wants to say to us today which is a word of salvation.

The Rule is imbued with the Word of God. Even though it is brief, it contains about 100 Scriptural allusions either explicit or implicit. St. Albert clearly was a man who had meditated at length on the Word of God. The hermits were commanded to meditate on the law of the Lord day and night. The reason for this precept is directed towards the transformation of the individual in Christ. It is important to seek with the intellect what the Word means but even more important is that the Word itself is on our lips and in our hearts and accompanies our every action (Rule, 19).

At the beginning of the Rule, St. Albert says that everyone is called to live in the "obsequium Iesu Christi". Studies on the Rule have shown that it is not a simple list of regulations; in fact, comparing the sketch of the Christian community present in the Acts of the Apostles with the Rule, one notes many points of convergence and a similar logical structure. In Acts we find the following:-

"They devoted themselves to the apostles' teaching and fellowship, to the breaking of bread and the prayers...And all who believed were together and had all things in common..." (2, 42-47) and "Now the company of those who believed were of one heart and soul, and no-one said that any of the things which he possessed was his own, but they had everything in common." (4,32).

The hermits came from various parts of Europe to live in the land made sacred by the presence of Jesus and where he shed his blood for the redemption of the human race. Jesus Christ is at the centre of the Rule and of the life of each hermit. They desired to form a community of disciples, taking as their model the primitive Christian community. In order to accomplish this project, each individual must allow the law of God to take full possession of his heart. To stay awake in prayer is an essential attitude (Rule, 10) in order to be always ready for the Lord's coming to us. A community can be compared to an orchestra. Each instrument must be in harmony with all the others so that the whole orchestra can play the same tune.

Analogously in our communities, the spiritual state of each member affects the whole community.

Each hermit is to remain in the cell assigned to him by the prior. Often we are tempted to seek God everywhere except where we are but God comes to meet us in our present reality and it is for us to discover God's presence in the events of every day. St. Augustine said that he had wasted a great deal of time searching for God outside himself when all the time God was present in his inmost being.

The Rule speaks of praying the canonical hours (Rule,11). When we pray the psalms, we have the possibility of assimilating the way Jesus Himself thought and prayed. Later this section of the Rule was applied to the obligation to pray the Divine Office, which is the official prayer of the whole Church. Christ, the head of the Body, intercedes always for us before the throne of mercy, and we, as members of the Church, take part in this constant prayer of Christ. We are living members of the Body of Christ which is the Church and we pray for one another and for the whole world. Christ is the eternal Priest and in him we are a chosen race, a royal priesthood, a holy nation (1 Pet, 2,9). We have the duty to praise and thank God on behalf of the world and perhaps especially on behalf of those who never think of God. In the Divine Office, we take part in the heavenly liturgy which is the intimate relationship between the Father, Son and Holy Spirit. This prayer of the whole Church nourishes us and helps us grow spiritually. It is important to bring to the liturgy fervent hearts so that when we leave to go back to our "cell" as the Rule says, the prayer of each of us will have been nourished by the prayer of the whole Church.

The hermits are to construct a chapel in the midst of their cells (Rule, 14) where they are to gather each morning to celebrate Eucharist. At the time the Rule was written it seems that hermits normally only gathered together for Mass on a Sunday and so the precept to gather each day points to the great importance which the first group of Carmelites gave to the Eucharist. The daily gathering is an invitation to come out of the solitude of the individual cells, and the risk of self-sufficiency, to meet with God in the heart of the community. We must make space in our lives to meet God face to face but we must never forget that the authenticity of any religious experience is proved in the way we relate to our neighbour. Does our personal prayer make us more able to accept other people as they are? God accepts us as we are in all our weakness and imperfection. Can we do the same with others?

The Eucharist is the celebration of the children of God. Before communion we receive the peace of Christ and we share this peace with one another. Thus united we are in communion with one another. We receive Christ in order to grow in His likeness as individuals and as community. By receiving communion we enter into union with Christ. The Rule helps us continue to live in union with Christ and in communion with one another so that together we may live in Him. The Eucharist is central to our prayer. During the celebration we make a formal offering of ourselves in union with Christ to the Father and after the celebration we must seek to put this formal offering into practice in daily life. The details of the Rule provide the structure within which we can do this and God presents us each day with many situations in which we can live out this offering. Obviously if we were aware in a particular moment that God was speaking to us in and through some event, we would listen carefully but God has become one of us and so approaches us every day in very human ways. Often the way God chooses to approach us is so insignificant that we have great difficulty recognising His presence. The solitude and silence of the cell is the sacred space where our hearts are tuned in to hear the voice of God. Through our personal and community prayer we learn how to listen to the still small voice of God who speaks within us and we learn to see God's face in the face of our neighbour.

According to the times and the place where the Rule was written, the spiritual life is seen as a combat between good and evil. Fasting and abstinence are proposed as a preparation for this great battle (Rule, 16 & 17). We must put on the armour of God (Rule, 19) and protect ourselves from every evil with the shield of faith.

We see in the life of St. Thérèse of Lisieux that her faith gave her the strength to continue despite great temptations. Faith involves believing firmly in the presence of God who lives in us and sustains us each moment. If we are in the desert or in the midst of darkness, it is faith in the living God which protects us and keeps us going. We are asked to put on the helmet of salvation to remind us of our need for salvation; we cannot save ourselves. We need to trust in the mercy of God who will liberate us from sin and lead us to eternal life. The sword of the Spirit, which is the Word of God, must abound in our mouths and hearts. We must seek to know the Word of God so that it will become an integral part of our being. We must be transformed by the Word so that the plan of God may be realised in each one of us. Reading and meditating on the Word of God will not necessarily make us learned people but will make us wise, filled with the wisdom of God which, to the eyes of the world, may appear to be foolishness but in reality this foolishness of God is wiser than all human wisdom and God's weakness is stronger than human strength (1 Cor. 1,25).

Work and silence are important parts of the Carmelite life. To work is to play a part in the creativity of God and so our work, whatever it may be, is important. However work must not become an idol for us; it is vital to make space for God in the midst of all our activities. Silence is the ambience in which we can more easily become aware of the presence of God. Silence should not just be an absence of noise; it must be filled with God. Exterior silence is useful but more necessary still is interior silence. In the silence of our hearts we can begin to discern the voice of God.

> "God spoke one word, which was His Son, and He always repeats it in an eternal silence, and in silence must it ever be heard by the soul." (John of the Cross, Maxims and Counsels, 21).

The first group of Carmelite hermits has blossomed into the world-wide Carmelite family. Being members of one family is a very important element of our Carmelite vocation. We do not follow Christ as isolated individuals but as sisters and brothers. There are obviously different ways of living this value of fraternity according to our particular calling. However the essential element is that we are aware that we are bound to one another as brothers and sisters. The heart of the Christian vocation is to become like Christ and to love as God loves. We can all be very good at loving our neighbour in theory; it is really loving real people which causes us problems. On our journey through the desert and up the slopes of Mount Carmel, we walk with other people who share our fundamental values and who are trying to follow Christ as we are. I think of our relationship with other people as God's gift to us. It is like the statue of the Pietá in St. Peter's. This started out as a block of marble and only Michelangelo could see what this block of marble would become. He started work on it using hammer and chisel. God is the great artist. God can see what we can become and so works on us. The tools which God uses are very often other people and especially those with whom we come into contact every day. They are the ones who rub away our rough corners.

We are unique individuals but we share a common heritage. We are bound together as brothers and sisters. We seek the face of God together and we find God in and through one another. Our love for God is proved by the way we treat one another. Our normal tendency is to restrict our love in some way but as we seek God together, we gradually learn to love from the Source of all love. As we let go of our narrow vision of who deserves to be loved, we learn to look at people as God looks at them. We learn compassion and respect for others and they begin to be set free by our love.

Being united as an international family is in itself a prophetic way of living. One of the essential elements of the Carmelite way of life is a commitment to serve others.. There are innumerable ways of doing this in daily life. All Christian service is somehow directed towards the coming of God's Kingdom. We seek to live the values of the Kingdom here and now and with our strong Elijan tradition, we are aware that we do so in a prophetic way. A prophet is one who proclaims the Word of God in particular situations. We can do this is very humble and unobtrusive ways as well as in very important works. Elijah was impelled to prophetic action because of his experience of God. The core of the Carmelite way of life is the contemplative dimension. Being a contemplative does not necessarily mean spending many hours in prayer each day, although a commitment to spending time alone with God is essential. The test of whether our experience of God is authentic is how we live in daily life – how we treat other people – whether we seek to serve others or not.

Titus Brandsma said that the Carmelite vocation is to become another Mary and I think that this sums up our contemplative vocation best of all. She had the most intimate relationship with Christ.

She let go of her own will, her own ideas and plans so that the will of God could be accomplished in her. Some people have difficulty with the way Catholics treat Our Lady and they point out how little she appears in the Gospels but this is precisely the way of a contemplative who becomes filled with God and points always towards God and away from herself.

Being a contemplative does not mean having extraordinary experiences in prayer. This happens to a very, very small number of people. Most contemplatives follow Christ through the desert in the night and rarely glimpse what is happening to them but God is at work in the darkness, forming and shaping them into a new creation. Article 17 of the Constitutions of the friars tells us that contemplation begins when we entrust ourselves to God *whatever way God chooses to come to us*. God often comes to us in totally unexpected ways. Mary received the Word of God through the message of an angel but she was also open to hearing God's voice at the foot of the cross. Elijah met God not in the earthquake or the fire or the mighty wind but in the sound of a gentle breeze. We must seek to be attentive for the voice of God in our daily lives.

Clearly there are many aspects to our Carmelite vocation but I am convinced that the contemplative aspect is crucial because if we take it seriously, the other aspects will also become much more fruitful. Carmel is synonymous with prayer and contemplation. We fulfil our vocation not by doing many things for God but allowing God to transform us.

If we accept the invitation of God to continue this interior journey, we will of course encounter some difficulties because we will begin to see more clearly what is motivating us. We will become aware that sometimes even our seemingly best actions emerge from selfish motives. However in following this path we will live out the fundamental values of our Rule and our spirituality and thus our human ways of thinking, loving and acting will be transformed into divine ways. We will see finally with the eyes of God and we will love the whole of creation with the heart of God.

For almost 800 years the Rule has inspired innumerable people to clothe themselves with the Word of God. Carmelite spirituality is not completely contained in the brief text of the Rule but it is the source from which the whole tradition emerges. I pray that our Rule be a living word for all of us and that it will inspire us today and in the future so that we will be worthy to follow in the footsteps of all those men and women throughout the ages who have taken the Rule as a light for their path.

FREEDOM UNDER AUTHORITY

"For freedom you have been set free. Do not submit again to the yoke of slavery." (Gal. 5,1). The desire to be free is not a modern invention. It has always existed in the hearts of men and women. The mission of Jesus was to set people free, to give them the freedom of the children of God.

If we see authority as the enemy of our freedom, then clearly we are going to have difficulties. The vow of obedience and the exercise of Christian authority are supposed to help all of us to be truly free. In the mendicant tradition, the prior, at every level, local prior, prior provincial, prior general, is the one who reminds the brothers of their common vocation; who constantly calls them to fidelity. He of course must first of all remind himself.

In the late sixties and early seventies, many changes were made in religious life in the wake of Vatican II. I never knew the pre-Vatican II religious life but I have heard many of the stories. Religious life was in need of a radical overhaul and many people responded with vigour. There was a great deal of confusion and many left religious life. The changes requested by the Council were very far reaching and perhaps many people thought that they had complied by dropping the habit and so on. However the fundamental change in religious life requested by the Council was that each religious order go back to its sources and rediscover its raison-d'être so that it could be re-interpreted for a new era.

After years of darkness and confusion, of uncertainty, debate and scholarly work, the Order returned to our sources and has managed to restate the Carmelite charism in modern terms. We seek to live a life of allegiance to Jesus Christ and to serve him faithfully. We do this by committing ourselves to the search for the face of the living God (the contemplative dimension of the Gospel), to fraternity and to service in the midst of the people (art 14). The experience of the desert is the unifying factor of these values (art. 15). The prophet Elijah and Our Lady are especially inspirational to us (art.25 ff). Of course the supreme norm for us and for every religious Order is the Gospel.

The charism is a gift which God has entrusted to the Carmelite Family and which has been handed down throughout the centuries. It is rather like a ball of wax which bears the impression of all who have handled it. We too will leave an impression of our hands and it is our duty to pass the ball on to others. This charism has inspired thousands of people throughout the ages and continues to inspire thousands today. The charism is not a narrow and restrictive thing but a life giving inspiration which has a great deal of room for all sorts of possibilities.

The vitality of the Rule has been rediscovered in the past twenty years or so as a fundamental inspiration for our way of life. The Constitutions, passed at the 1995 General Chapter, are the authentic expression of the charism as it is understood in our day. Most Provinces of the Order have organised days so that the members can deepen their understanding of the charism as expressed in the Constitutions. At the General Chapter, it was felt that we have done enough agonising over who we are. We have grown beyond that stage and now our task is to look at how we must incarnate this charism in each culture.

In the Constitutions we are reminded that Jesus lived his freedom not in self-sufficiency but in obedience to the Father. Jesus obeyed because he loved the Father and because he loved us (45). Therefore the context of obedience is love. Religious obedience is understood by the same article of the Constitutions as a surrender of our will fully to God. As we follow the obedient, poor and chaste Christ, we become less focused on ourselves (43). Article 46 tells us that following Christ in his obedience means listening together to the word of God and reading the signs of the times in order to discern the will of God today. Doing this, however, involves a constant and profound process of transformation.

Undergoing the process of transformation is not easy. Our freedom has been won at great cost - Christ's death on the cross - and he tells all those who follow him, that they too must be prepared to die - for those who wish to save their life, will lose it but those who lose their life for his sake and for the sake of the Gospel will keep it for the eternal life. To become truly free we need to follow Christ to the cross and beyond. For many, freedom comes at too great a cost and they find slavery more congenial. To be free involves letting go of the old self which is self absorbed in order to receive our true self as a gift from God. We are slaves when we are driven by our hidden needs and desires and when these become absolute demands brooking no interference from the legitimate needs and rights of others.

What is crucial is our motivation. All the writings of John of the Cross about the dark nights refers to the transformation process whereby an individual grows from selfishness to pure love. The word which John uses for good people, good religious, who say their prayers and live good lives is "beginners" and he paints a devastating picture of them. He points out that though on the surface they appear to be very good in fact their motivation is all wrong and you just have to scratch the surface and you will see a different side to their character.

So in relation to the exercise of our freedom, what is our motivation? If our motivation is to adhere totally to Christ and consent to God's will in our lives, then we are free. A problem arises when an unfree individual desires to exercise his freedom and this brings him into conflict with another unfree individual who has authority. Could it be that we are driven by our own needs and are not in fact inspired by the pure love of God? Could it be that some selfishness creeps in to our exercise of freedom and authority? Could it be that we are not free at all?

This is why the Constitutions speak of the necessity of transformation in order to live out our vow of obedience (46). If we want to continue doing our own thing undisturbed and have no interest in consenting to God's purifying action in our lives, then we really are wasting our time discussing this because nothing is going to change.

We show that we consent to God's purifying action in our lives by doing our part to dismantle the false and selfish part of us. We cannot accomplish this work on our own; it does require God's power because our selfishness is so deep rooted. The first step towards dismantling the selfish part of us which enslaves us is to try to get below the surface and examine our motives for our actions. Our emotions are our greatest friends in that they infallibly point to our true values despite what we may say or think. They tell us what is really going on inside us.

If I am asked to be assistant pastor in a parish and I angrily refuse it, I need to examine the reasons for my anger. Why did I react to a simple request by becoming angry? Did I feel insulted that I was not asked to be the pastor? Did I feel neglected and rejected by the whole Province and therefore reacted by refusing to countenance the request? There is nothing at all wrong with those feelings. It is normal and human to feel things like that. I exercise maturity and freedom when I can look at my motives honestly, accept what I feel and then make a rational decision based on the evidence. I am a slave when my feelings force me to act in a particular way and then I use my rational powers to find reasons to back up my childish stance.

It should be obvious that simply because I do or do not want to do something, it does not necessarily follow that God must want the same thing. If Jesus had followed that principle, he would have run as fast as he could from the garden of Gethsemane. If you are determined to do your own thing come what may then again you are wasting time looking at this subject. It is only worthwhile discussing this if you really are searching for God's will and willing to examine your motives.

What is the point of offering God one thing when He is asking something completely different from us? How do we know what God's will is for us? This is obviously a very complex issue and we can never be certain that we have got it right either as individuals or as communities. However God writes straight with crooked lines and can use our mistakes and even our sins to bring about something good. We can only do our best and try to discern what is God's will. If we genuinely try to discern, then I do not believe we will go far wrong.

Discernment of course involves taking account of what God puts in front of our faces. We cannot claim to be discerning if we pay no attention to the Gospel, which is the supreme norm for all Christians, or the Rule and Constitutions, which are the authentic inspiration of Carmelite life in our day.

The exercise of freedom is Christian when it is not driven by self-ish motives but when we make decisions taking into account not just how we feel and what we want but also all the other relevant circumstances and then make decisions which we believe are for the building up of the Kingdom of God and not our own little kingdom. The crucial factor is our motivation – what really lies behind our decisions.

LEADERSHIP AND RESPONSIBILITY

The role of the Prior in our Rule and tradition is one of service. He leads the community first of all by his own example and his task is to make sure that the community is organised in such a way that the brothers can live a life of allegiance to Jesus Christ and serve him with a stout heart and a good conscience. Several times in the Rule it states that the Prior is to make certain decisions with the consent of the other brothers or at least of the more mature and saner part! The Prior is not a despot or a parent who is to decide everything for his children. He is a leader but each member of the community is responsible for the health of the whole community and for his own life. The Prior is the one who is to remind all the brothers of our common vocation and constantly to recall all of us to that. However each one is ultimately responsible before God for how he actually lives the vocation which God has given him.

The theme of leadership and responsibility is very much connected with that of freedom and authority and also that of community. An essential part of the Carmelite charism as it is understood in our Constitutions is a commitment to community. I am very aware that in most Provinces of the Order there are several Carmelites who live outside a recognised Carmelite community and there are many reasons for such a situation. It may not be the ideal but it is possible for someone who lives outside a Carmelite community to be more committed to community than one who lives inside.

I remind you of Constitution number 35:-

Each community shall comprise a sufficient number of friars to create an appropriate environment in which a truly fraternal life can develop. Any friar who, for reasons of health, study, or apostolate, or for some other legitimate motive, must live outside his house, shall be attached to a well-established community, whose members shall encourage a fraternal relationship, assisting him in his activities. For his part, as far as he can, he shall visit the community on a regular basis, and shall willingly take part in some of the community's meetings, in order to benefit more fully from the advantages of brotherhood.

The reality is often very different from the theory. The role of leadership is to move the reality as close as possible to the ideal while being guided above all by the requirements of charity. Some, and perhaps many of our communities, are not an appropriate environment in which a truly fraternal life can develop. That is the reality. What are we going to do about it?

There are various possible reactions. We could just get on with our work and our lives whilst trying our best to live fraternally in community. In this case we would attend prayers in common and meetings etc but what gives us life may very well be outside the community. Another possible reaction is to remain within a community but be constantly angry at the complete ineptitude of the Provincial and Council for its failure to do anything about the situation of community life in the Province (or lack of it). We could withdraw altogether from community life for a variety of motives - too difficult, loss of commitment, anger at some perceived slight and so on.

We believe that a vocation comes from God but we must admit that mixed in with a divine call is the human element. So we find all sorts of people in religious communities. Some should never have become religious as they are totally unsuited to community life; others have been embittered by the harsh experiences of everyday life and are never really happy no matter how many good things happen to them; others are suffering under various kinds of illnesses or addictions; others, who do most of the work in any Province, are trying their best to respond to what they believe God is asking of them. Like everyone else they are limited, make mistakes, commit sin and so on.

A group of religious is a microcosm of the Church and the world. A vital part of the human response to a vocation is an acceptance of these concrete people with all their faults and failings. I would suggest that if this acceptance is not present, then our vows are invalid. Decrees of nullity are granted to people who married without having the maturity to appreciate what that involved. When we make our profession in the Order we take on community as an integral part of our vocation. This means that we have thrown in our lot with this group for better for worse, for richer for poorer, in sickness and in health till death do us part.

Each Provincial community has certain apostolic works which have either been inherited from long tradition or taken on in recent years. As a member of a Provincial community, you are responsible for these works. The supreme legislative body within a Province is the Chapter. It is here that you make decisions about your future and you have to own these decisions. You can decide to close certain apostolates but if you vote for the Province to have ten parishes, a school etc etc, who is going to staff these? Abstaining is a perfectly reasonable way to vote if we have no particular opinion about the topic or cannot make up our minds. It is not reasonable if it is a refusal to take responsibility and to remain aloof from the Province. Are you prepared to give up your own position in order to go to one of the Provincial apostolates? Are you prepared to go along with the direction of the Province over the next few years? If not why not? What is motivating you?

You will elect a Provincial and Council to represent you and they have certain authority to act in your name. It is not usual for everyone to agree with every decision that is taken but as members of the Province, we have to decide whether we can live with what has been decided or whether it does such violence to our conscience that we have no option but to leave the Province and seek incardination elsewhere either in another Province or as a diocesan priest. Being freelance is a very attractive option to many of us but it is neither one thing nor the other. Elijah challenged the people to stop hobbling first on one leg then on the other and I would say the same - choose whether you want to belong to the Provincial community or not. If you do, throw in your lot with the others. You cannot live for very long with other human beings without being hurt in some way. That is part of life but should not be used as an excuse to walk away from the community, retaining the privileges of a member of the Province but accepting none of the responsibilities.

Sometimes in a Chapter we can get carried away by enthusiasm and pass all sorts of decrees which have no chance of being put into effect. This causes disillusion among the brothers so I would plead with you to be realistic. At the same time it is good to have a bit of vision and try to set some reasonable goals for the Province, something which the majority are willing to work towards together. However realism is also important when formulating a vision. It may be that our goals seem very modest but if they are achieved this will give the whole group confidence to go forward and plan other goals.

What future do you want to construct for the Provincial community? Are you willing to be part of this future? One definition of the Carmelite charism is to form praying communities at the service of Godís people. What does that mean in the concrete reality of your Province? Are you willing to move, to change your way of doing things in order to fit in with how the group wants to go forward?

Obviously whoever you choose as leaders are not going to be as visionary as you, or as intelligent! They are going to be very limited. They are going to make certain decisions about the Province and some of these might appear to you to be very mistaken. I think that ideally everyone should have an opportunity to serve as Provincial or at least as Councillor, then there would be far fewer criticisms of those in leadership positions! Many of the decisions which are made by Provincial Councils are forced on them by circumstances beyond their control. When the minutes are published the real reason for the decision is not stated because to do so would be to publicise the hidden faults of an individual and to do so would be uncharitable and so the members of the Council are open to criticism for deciding to do X instead of Y and perhaps only they know that in fact they had no choice but to make the decision.

The reality in which we find ourselves is far from ideal. Some people spend their whole adult lives in the search for the ideal place or the ideal apostolate and the sad thing is they never find it. They end up bitter and disillusioned blaming God, life, the Church, the Order, Provincials, the brethren but never ever themselves. I believe totally in ideals. We have the Carmelite ideals presented to us in the Rule and Constitutions which guide us on our journey but this journey is long and difficult. It is such a temptation to give up the journey and settle for mediocrity. If however we seek to continue the journey we will learn a lot about ourselves and this revelation will make us much more understanding and accepting of the faults and foibles of others because we will know profoundly the areas where we are not completely mature.

In order to reach the goal of the journey we need to consent to the purifying action of God in our lives which comes to us in the events of everyday. As we advance on this journey, we become more and more mature. Maturity and wisdom does not come automatically with age unfortunately but only when we allow the experience of life to change us; when we listen to the still small voice of God who speaks to us from the midst of daily life. To seek to avoid responsibility is to remain immature. Remember the story of those who received the talents and they risked these in order to earn more but one refused to accept the risk and buried his in the ground in order to hand it back in pristine condition to the master. The master was not well pleased.

Each of us has been given many talents and we have been called to bring these together for a community enterprise. Those who are called to the service of leadership have certain responsibilities for which they must answer but their role does not take away from the responsibility of the rest of the group. You are all responsible for the future. What future are you going to build for Carmel in our Provinces?

PLANNING FOR THE FUTURE

The General Chapter 1995 seems a distant memory now but it will continue to affect us for many years to come. The final document from that Chapter contains many of the insights which emerged during the meeting. Also the Constitutions which we approved at the Chapter are the fruit of many years of reflection within the Order as a whole. They describe very well what our vocation is and they encourage us to live it in ever greater depth.

The General Chapter asked the newly elected General Council to produce a global plan for its work over the following six years. This was done and was discussed at the Council of Provinces 1997, held in Lisieux. In this document, the Council declared its wish to continue the work of the previous General Council regarding the Carmelite Family and working with the Discalced Carmelites. There are now several letters written jointly by the two Superiors General to both Orders. We wish to encourage the various ways in which the two Orders are working together in many parts of the world.

In the plan of the General Council we speak of the need for each one of us to pray ardently and work unceasingly so that new vocations will come to us. The best thing we can do is to live our own vocation to the full. We also wish to work for a new missionary spirit in the Order and we have been very pleased with the new foundations which have been made and will be made during the six years since the General Chapter 1995. There are huge areas of the world which wait to hear the Gospel of Christ. Our Carmelite charism has a great deal to offer the world and we are responsible for making it available to others. The Church is missionary by nature and we must be prepared to play our part in this essential work of the Church.

Underpinning all the work of the General Council is a desire to encourage a renewal of the contemplative aspect of our charism. We are the inheritors of a great tradition which stretches back about 800 years. The Carmelite charism is a gift from the Holy Spirit to the Church for the world. We do not own the charism but by our lives we are meant to enhance it, enrich it and pass it on to others.

We have been called to live the Gospel according to the Carmelite way and we are most faithful to the Gospel when we are faithful to our Carmelite tradition. Our Rule is imbued with the Word of God. The two figures who inspire us most of all after Christ Himself are two biblical figures – the prophet Elijah and Mary, the mother of Jesus. So the Word of God is central to our way of life. It is where we find our inspiration. It is the life-giving word of life for us. St. Jerome said that the one who ignores the Scriptures ignores Christ. Lectio Divina has been rediscovered within the Carmelite Family as an efficacious way of prayer, the purpose of which is to lead us into an intimate relationship with God. Lectio cannot be limited to reading the Word of God or thinking about it or discussing its meaning, although all these are important. There is a time when words fail and only silence is an appropriate response to God's Word. It is wonderful when a community reads the Word of God together and discusses the implications of this Word for personal and community growth. It is also important to let go of our own thoughts, ideas and opinions and simply listen to God in a deep silence. Listening to God in silence together is a powerful means of growing in our community relationships.

A religious vocation is also a gift from God to particular individuals. I believe that a true vocation is when an individual discovers gradually the Carmelite within him or her. For this to take place the individual must encounter the Carmelite charism particularly in Carmelites. The charism is one way of following Christ; it is our way. Like other Christians we have been called to follow Christ and bear witness to him by living the Gospel in daily life. The Gospel is of course so rich that no-one or no group could ever exhaust it by any particular way of life. The Gospel has inspired and continues to inspire very many initiatives including the Carmelite way. It seems that a normal life span for a religious congregation is about 200 years. Why some continue for much longer is hard to say but it surely has something to do with the particular charism expressing something essential to the Gospel. Some congregations were founded to do a particular work and when the need for this work diminished so did the need for the congregation. There is of course no particular Carmelite work but we express our Carmelite vocation in various fields of activity. So long as we live the vocation given us by God the Carmelite Family will continue in existence.

As Carmelites we are heirs to a long contemplative tradition which we cannot ignore if we are to be faithful to the vocation given us by God. We cannot leave contemplation to the enclosed communities while we concentrate on ministry which is also an important part of our vocation. Contemplation, community and service in the midst of the people are three vital elements of our charism which cannot be separated. According to our Constitutions, they are united by the experience of the desert.

We are usually committed to ministry and are good at it. We serve the people well in our parishes, schools, retreat centres etc and we can get affirmation from our work. Also we tend to be committed, at least in theory to community. However there comes a time when we meet with difficulties in our ministry and/or in community. Without the contemplative dimension of our charism, we tend to meet these difficulties on a purely human level and react very humanly by fighting back or withdrawing according to our temperament. St. Therese of Lisieux looked at the difficulties of life as opportunities to exercise her vocation to be love. She was able to do this because she was a contemplative. She was not contemplative simply because she lived in an enclosed monastery but because she truly heard the Word of God in the depths of her heart and allowed this Word to transform her life totally. She continued to follow this life project even when she met with all sorts of difficulties because through her silent listening to the Word of God, she was able to see beyond the obvious and see God's hand at work in the midst of the situation in which she found herself.

Contemplation allows us to live community at a deeper level because we will understand that despite the difficulties of living together and all sorts of interpersonal problems, we are all one in Christ. Authentic   contemplation also leads to prophetic action as we are able to discern the true needs of people and serve them with a pure heart. The ability to let go of our own thoughts, ideas and opinions and listen to God in the silence of our hearts leads inevitably to listening to people with the heart and not only with our physical ears. We also will be drawn to listening to the poor because through our contemplation we can see beyond externals.

Service and community require a great deal of effort from us. The same is true for the contemplative aspect of our vocation. We will not be contemplatives unless we pray. This takes time and a great deal of effort because listening does not come naturally to us. Prayer is the face to face encounter with the Living God. It is the relationship with God which will lead to union with God if we consent. We have so many ways of avoiding this encounter because it does involve the need to change and we tend not to like that. So we use all of our ingenuity to avoid the need to change. We can be so busy with ministry that we have no time for prayer or we can keep prayer at a very superficial level.

A Dutch artist has made a very beautiful version of the Rule. At the centre of the Rule there is a golden circle with an empty centre. This empty centre is meant to signify the human yearning for God. There is an empty space in our lives that can only be filled by God because the space is infinite. We usually try all sorts of ways to fill this space, ways which cannot ever satisfy us. Our vocation enables us to speak to this deep human need. From our experience we can help people see that God alone can satisfy the human heart but we must be able to speak from our own experience.

In recent years Carmelites have woken up to the importance of the Prophet Elijah for our lives and ministry. This has been an excellent development and reflection on him has helped us see the importance of combining contemplation and prophetic action. Also for centuries we have been known as Mary's Order. Some of our writers said that the reason we were founded was to continue the love which Jesus had for his mother during his earthly life. The scapular has of course summed up Carmelite devotion to Our Lady. She is for us both mother and sister. She is the mother of the divine life within us, teaching us by example the vital importance of listening to the Word of God and thus allowing it to take root in our lives. She was not only a hearer of the Word but also she put the Word into practice. As our sister she accompanies us on our journey of faith. She shared our human life and experienced joy and sorrow in abundant measure. The first title of Our Lady within the Carmelite Order was protectress. In faith we know that we are not alone but that we have the assistance of the communion of saints. By wearing the scapular and trying to live what this rich symbol signifies, we accept that we are under the protection of Our Lady and we must try to remember that in the busy reality of daily life.

Titus Brandsma wrote that the vocation of the Carmelite is to be another Mary. She was the God-bearer for the world. Her "yes" gave God space to come into the world in a new way. At her word God became incarnate. If, like her, we truly consent to the presence and action of God in our lives, the divine life will grow within us. This is the purifying and transforming process which is an essential part of the Christian life. We will then become God-bearers for our world and of course this will lead to some kind of prophetic action which need not be dramatic to the eyes of human beings but will be according to the heart of God. Expressing our devotion in ways which speak to the whole person is important but we also must not forget the necessity of living the reality which the devotion implies. We should show our love for Our Lady in various ways but we must include the practical imitation of her virtues.

Throughout the centuries the same Carmelite charism has been lived in many ways. What does our Carmelite vocation look like in our own particular culture and time and what will it look like in the future? All of us are responsible for giving an answer to that question in the way we choose to live our calling.

CARMEL IN THE WORLD

During my visits to the Carmelite Family throughout the world, I have come across many different customs and ways of understanding what it means to be a Carmelite but everywhere I have found the same Carmelite values. These values are well expressed in the Constitutions of the friars:-

"To live a life of allegiance to Jesus Christ and to serve him faithfully with a pure heart and a clear conscience":these words, inspired by St. Paul, are the basis for all the elements of our charism; they are the foundation upon which Albert constructed our way of life.

. . . .

Carmelites live their life of allegiance to Christ through a commitment to seek the face of the living God (the contemplative dimension of life), through fraternity, and through service in the midst of the people. (14)

There are many things to be pleased about as we look around the Order. Of course problems exist everywhere but on the whole and within our particular limitations we are dedicated to the "obsequium Jesu Christi". There has been in recent years an upsurge of interest in spirituality, especially our own Carmelite tradition. Much work and study has gone in to our history and many of the publications which have come from the Carmelite Institute in Rome and other institutes will be invaluable sources for further study. The Order has taken seriously Fr. Kilian Healy's plea for further study on the Rule and now we have several excellent books which have given us new ways of looking at this ancient document which has been rediscovered as a primary source of inspiration for all Carmelites. There has also been some solid research on our saints and mystics. Much more needs to be done but what has been accomplished so far is notable. The General Council wants to encourage higher studies and following the decision of the General Chapter 1995, we have appointed a Delegate for Culture.

The General Council wants to specially promote the study of mariology among us so we can deepen this very important aspect of our charism. There is a particular interest in the Order at present in biblical studies and that is wonderful to see because as was expressed in the final document of the General Chapter 1995, "To be zealous for the Word of God, to pray it, live it and proclaim it, is the priority for the Order for the next six years." (4.4)

As an integral part of this renewed interest in our spirituality has been a refounding of the ancient practice of Lectio Divina. In many communities throughout the world it is normal practice to have a time when all the members gather to read the Word of God together, meditate on it, respond to the Word in prayer and share a silent resting in this Word together. This practice cannot but help communities be united and even more apostolically fruitful. I want to strongly encourage this practice. Perhaps we need to remind ourselves however that Lectio is not simply talking about Scripture but soaking ourselves in the Word so that we become little by little transformed by this Word who is Christ.

We have taken risks and planted Carmel in other lands. We are well established in Brazil of course but also other parts of Latin America are showing signs of growth. We have recently made a foundation in Trinidad. In Africa we are also well established in Zimbabwe and the Democratic Republic of the Congo. We have recently established ourselves in Mozambique and we hope to make foundations also in Kenya, Tanzania and Burkina Faso.

Asia is where the greatest growth has taken place in recent years. Indonesia especially is witnessing a time when many vocations are presenting themselves. India also is growing rapidly and is now beginning to look outside Kerala for apostolic possibilities. The Philippines hopes to be an independent Commissariat or Province by the year 2000.

In Eastern Europe there is a certain growth taking place. We have celebrated 650 years of Carmelite presence in the Czech lands and 600 years in Poland. We have received a good number of vocations from Rumania and these are being nurtured by the Italian Province which hopes to make a foundation there as soon as circumstances permit. The plan is for various branches of the Carmelite Family to make foundations in the same area and to bear witness together to our fundamental Carmelite values. The Polish Province has a community in the Ukraine and perhaps one day we will go into Russia also.

The Church is missionary by nature and so must our Order be. The Provinces which have a missionary outreach outside their territory can bear witness to the new life which this can bring to the whole Province. I would urge those Provinces which do not as yet have some missionary outreach to seriously consider this possibility. Of course in many areas there is an acute shortage of vocations which is more or less severe according to the particular country. There are some signs of a possible resurgence of interest in the Religious Life but it does not look as if the vocations will come in the numbers they used to in days gone by. This fact necessitates some serious thought and planning for the future so that Provinces can adapt to changed circumstances. We can complain about the shortage of vocations or we can view this fact as a grace from God and an opportunity for an exercise of "creative fidelity". Creativity can also be exercised in how we approach mission. Perhaps the General Council can help here by co-ordinating a missionary project in the sense of bringing together two of more Provinces which can work together for a single project. I would remind you that God is never outdone in generosity. Perhaps we are like the poor widow of the Gospel who put into the Temple coffers all she had to live on. We will find that if we give, there will be gifts for us, a full measure, pressed down, shaken together shall be poured into our laps.

We have been called by the Church to take our part in the era of new evangelisation. Western Europe and the USA are just as much mission territory as anywhere else since we are living in a post-Christian age. The new evangelisation is new in its ardour, its methods and its expressions. What does this mean for us? We need to recommit ourselves to our Carmelite vocation and to find new ways to express the fundamental values of our life, ways which will communicate effectively to people of the third millennium.

Contemplation is an essential part of our charism. Art. 17 of the Constitutions of the friars tells us that contemplation is an attitude of openness to God whose presence we discover everywhere. Our

preaching or teaching or whatever work with which we are involved
does not bring Christ to people but hopefully helps them to discover
His presence in their lives or be more aware of it. Christ is already
present in each situation and individual before we arrive. Above all
our daily lives, our presence, should reveal something of God. Can
we really discover the presence of God everywhere even in difficulties? This is the faith of Our Lady in the Magnificat who praises
God for throwing down the proud, feeding the hungry and sending
the rich away empty when most people would see the opposite as
true. A contemplative is able to see beyond the externals to the reality beneath. A constant attitude of openness to God is of course not
easy because the presence of God calls into question how we live and
constantly calls us to conversion which means change and we are not
always very keen to change. Daily we need to renew our commitment to Jesus Christ and to urge all our brothers to do the same so
that we become a living page of the Gospel for our neighbours to
read. In this way we will take our part in the new evangelisation so
much desired by the Pope.

There are some wonderful things going on in the Order - things
to be proud of. Our Carmelite values are being spread to other lands
and most especially among lay people in the established Provinces.
We have now some excellent tools to help us continue our work,
notably our new Constitutions and the many scholarly works which
the Order has produced. However there are some areas in which all
of us could improve.

It is the task of the Prior General "to ensure effectively the common good of the whole Order; to work strenuously so that the
authentic spirit of Carmel, especially with respect to the life of
prayer, may be truly present in every Province, and increase day by
day; to promote tirelessly the growth and development of the Order
and the apostolic and academic vitality of the religious." (Constit.
275)

Despite the renewed interest in spirituality which finds expression
in the new Constitutions, I wonder whether it has really filtered down
to the community level and whether it is really expressed in practice.
In general during my visits I have found that we are excellent pastors
giving wonderful service in our parishes, schools, retreat centres etc.

We are most certainly hard workers but at times our work is at the expense of our community and prayer life. According to art. 64 of the Constitutions, prayer is the irremovable centre of our lives and actually makes possible authentic community and apostolic service. We need to work on all sorts of aspects of our life but I have been underlining the contemplative dimension of our charism wherever I have gone not because I do not see the other elements of our life as extremely important but simply that, in line with the Constitutions, I believe this aspect to be fundamental and indeed to be the source of our fraternal life and apostolic work.

As I visit the Provinces, I find that community prayer ranges from nothing at all to the full Office and daily Eucharist in common. Constitution no. 69 reminds us,

> As in the primitive Church, as religious we are called to celebrate together the Eucharist and the Liturgy of the Hours. Liturgical prayer is the highest form of communal encounter with God, and brings about what it celebrates. Personal prayer is intimately linked with liturgical prayer; one flows from the other.

I am not so much concerned with the amount of Divine Office we say together as with the quality of our prayer. This lies not in our words or even our holy thoughts but in our intention. God reads our hearts and of course it is perfectly possible for the lips to say "yes" and for the heart to say "no". It is not those who say, "Lord, Lord" who will enter the Kingdom of heaven but those who do the will of the Father. According to art. 17 of our Constitutions,

> contemplation is the inner journey of Carmelites, arising out of the free initiative of God, who touches and transforms us, leading us towards unity of love with him, raising us up so that we may enjoy this gratuitous love and live in his loving presence.

It is a transforming experience of the overpowering love of God. This love empties us of our limited and imperfect human ways of thinking, loving, and behaving, transforming them into divine ways

Is that really our desire? Is it what we really intend or is it just beautiful words? For example do the members of our Provinces and Commissariats go on an annual retreat? (Do we?) If they do, is it for a more intimate encounter with the One whom we know loves us or to get good ideas for future homilies. Remember also the injunction in the Constitutions regarding the need to dedicate an adequate time each day to silent prayer (art. 80). My impression is that many of us are too busy for this practice. While of course it is laudable to serve the Lord in all our many apostolic activities, we need to continually remember who is the source of all apostolic fruitfulness. It is understandable that we often prefer activity to prayer because it tends to be more gratifying but activity without prayer will sooner or later become empty. Liturgical and personal prayer is an absolute essential in order that the salt retain its flavour.

Community life is another difficult issue in Religious Life as a whole. While there is a deep thirst for community in our world, real community is not easy to live. It makes great demands on us but also gives us a great deal in return. There are many ways to live community but whatever way we live it, community should provide an atmosphere in which each member can feel accepted and grow as a human being and as a member of the Order. Fraternity is an essential aspect of our Carmelite vocation. Living this value helps each individual to grow as a human being, a Christian and a Carmelite and also bears witness to our world that real community is possible despite human differences. Community makes demands on us but we receive much in return.

A charism is a gift given by God for the Church and the world. The Carmelite charism has a very rich and long history. We are the inheritors of a great tradition. We are responsible for enriching this tradition by the witness of our own lives and for passing on this charism, which we have received as stewards, to others.

A CONTEMPLATIVE COMMUNITY IN THE MIDST OF THE PEOPLE

We are the brothers of the Blessed Virgin Mary of Mount Carmel. Our Order began because the Latin hermits on Mount Carmel wanted to form themselves into a community of brothers. They had been together long enough to work out for themselves a proposal for a way of life which they took to St. Albert, Patriarch of Jerusalem, so that he could give them ecclesiastical approval. When Albert's "formula vitae" was formally approved as a Rule by Pope Innocent IV in 1247, the hermits were inscribed in the new mendicant movement which was sweeping Europe at the time. The Carmelite hermits became Carmelite friars called to the service of the people. One of the hallmarks of the mendicants was that they lived in the midst of the people and not in large monasteries like the monks.

Despite the fact that the Order is clearly called to the active apostolate, contemplation remains a fundamental element of our vocation. We understand ourselves to be contemplative communities at the service of God's people in whose midst we live. Thank God we have passed beyond those years when we were still searching for our identity. Our identity is now clear. What remains for us is to tease out the implications of our charism for our daily life.

We are to live a life of allegiance to Jesus Christ and to serve him faithfully with a pure heart and a clear conscience and we do this through a commitment to seek the face of the living God (the contemplative dimension of life), through fraternity, and through service (diakonia) in the midst of the people. (Constitution, 14). These three elements are closely interwoven being bound together by the experience of the desert which is the experience of the purifying action of God in our lives. Contemplation determines the quality of our fra-

ternal life and of our service in the midst of the people of God
(Constitution, 18). The goal of contemplation is to be transformed
in God and thus see reality with the eyes of God and love with the
heart of God (Cf. Constitution, 15).

A contemplative attitude allows us to discover the presence of
God in others and to appreciate the mystery of those with whom we
share our lives (Constitution, 19). We are called to community, to
share our lives with others but above all with our brothers and this in
itself is a witness to others that God is present in our midst and
through this witness God will touch the hearts of many.

We could speak very beautifully about the theory of community
and its theological meaning but we all know that the reality of religious community is very different. Our communities mirror the reality of the Church and of the world in which we live. We are
redeemed sinners who are striving to do the will of God. We are not
perfect as individuals and therefore we cannot have perfect communities yet.

There is a thirst for community in our world and yet at the same
time individualism is rampant. This tension is present in our own
lives since we cannot but be affected by the world in which we live.
We are drawn to community on the one hand but on the other we are
tempted to put our own needs and desires above everything else and
to judge everything by how it affects us. Community is not easy and
though we are committed to living community, it is crucial to recognise the tendency which exists in all of us to escape its demands and
to close in on ourselves in selfishness. This is the reality of sin in our
lives but we have been redeemed. Clearly the redemption won for us
by Christ has not made saints of us yet; we are hopefully on the way.
Christ offers us a way to grow beyond our limitations but we must
accept the healing which he offers. The first stage of healing is to
recognise that something is not quite right.

What is it like to live in our Carmelite communities? "The community of believers were of one heart and one mind. None of them
ever claimed anything as his own; rather everything was held in common." (Acts. 4,32). If that is your experience of community life, you
are truly blessed but I would guess that this is not your experience. I
would guess that at best it is reasonably pleasant and that in your

community you have come to a mutual acceptance of one another. At worst ..it can be very difficult and a reality from which we seek to escape at every opportunity. Why is our community not perfect? We can blame the Provincial and Council for putting us in this dreadful situation or for dumping Brother X on the community or we can blame our brothers with whom it is impossible to form true community despite our desire to do so. We could try blaming God of course but if we find ourselves blaming everyone but ourselves perhaps this should ring a warning bell for us. Could it be possible that others find us difficult to live with and in their hearts are blaming us for the lack of real community?

We have been called together from many different backgrounds. We come into community with our own particular experience of life which has marked us for good or for ill. We approach community with our own baggage and our often very different expectations. We may use the same word, "community", but we may mean very different things. I believe that the first step towards improving our community life is to accept that we are different and that we may be looking for different things. We need to accept one another in all our diversity and try to see in this human reality something of the richness of God. Each individual truly is a mystery. We need to accept the fact that some individuals are so badly damaged by the ups and downs of life that they are almost completely dysfunctional. Where their behaviour is damaging to the community life, they must be challenged and every help given to them to live a more balanced life. I appreciate that this is no easy task but failure to challenge inappropriate behaviour leads to the dysfunctional individual dominating the life of the community. Such people are in a minority but all of us need to be challenged from time to time to be faithful to the vocation to which we have been called. This challenge can come to us very often through the daily living with others. We preach the Gospel but the test of our words is in our deeds. It is very easy to love our neighbour if we do not have a neighbour. How we actually live in community will tell us whether we really are men of prayer and will tell others. The authenticity of our prayer will become obvious through our daily contact with our brothers.

Although living the reality of community is not easy, it is the way which God has chosen for us. If vocation is not something imposed on us from the outside but part of our inner reality which we discover little by little, then the yearning for community and the ability to live it is written into the very fabric of our being. Of course because of our fallen nature, we have things out of balance but the elements of community life can help us to grow if we are willing to follow Christ into the desert.

There is no gain without pain. Growing up is painful but the pain forms us into mature men. There is a serious danger in religious life of remaining immature all our lives. We receive what we need from the community whether we work for it or not. If we are awkward enough, we will be given anything we want just to keep us happy and so that the others can have some peace. Then we are just like spoiled children. Following Christ leads inevitably to the cross in some form or another. This is not a punishment but God's way of helping us become what He knows we can be. Through our experience of life, God will purify us, rubbing away our rough corners. We will probably not appreciate it at the time but the end result makes it very worthwhile. Some of this purifying will take place in and through our life in community. Are we willing to consent to the action of God in our lives or will we turn away and instead do what we want? This is the difference between working for God and doing God's work. Working for God means to do what we want and we assume that it also must be what God wants. Doing God's work can be very different - doing what God is really asking of us which involves us in careful discernment and silent listening for the still small voice of God who speaks to us through the most unexpected people.

The Constitutions point out those elements of our life which are designed to help us grow as individuals and as brothers (31). The first is "in the shared participation in the Eucharist, through which we become one body, and which is the source and the summit of our lives, and therefore the sacrament of brotherhood." Do we have a shared Eucharist in our communities? This is written into our Rule and was a very unusual precept for hermits. I am not proposing a shared Eucharist because it is part of our law but because it is the greatest help we have to build up our communities. I am well aware that there can be all sorts of reasons why community Eucharist is not convenient but where there is a will, there is a way. Sometimes the demands of the apostolate can be used as an excuse to escape other demands. In this case we need to look at our lives with great honesty. What am I seeking? What do I want to do with my life and what does God want of me? How does my lifestyle fit in with my vocation to be a Carmelite?

The second element mentioned in the Constitutions is similar to the first, that is the communal celebration of the Liturgy of the Hours. Perhaps some of us are still suffering from the experience of the past where in some cases the community said lots of prayers together but the individual members could not stand one another. Prayer can be used to boost our own ego instead of being an opening to the purifying and healing action of God but that danger is not a reason to give up prayer either as individuals or as communities. St. Teresa of Avila said that with regard to prayer we need to have a very determined determination to keep going and never give up. If we want to praise God together as brothers, the Church has given us a precious opportunity to do so by means of the Liturgy of the Hours whereby we join with the whole Church to offer to God the sacrifice of praise. It is of course possible to enliven our liturgical celebrations so that they do not became routine.

The next element mentioned in the Constitutions for the building up of our community life is the prayerful listening to the Word. This of course is part of the celebration of the Eucharist and of the Liturgy of the Hours but is also recommended by means of Lectio Divina where together we read and reflect on the Word of God and share our response to this Word in our own words and in silence where we allow the Word to shape our hearts and to bind us together in unity. We cannot have prayerful communities if we are not prayerful individuals. Each one of us is responsible for the health of the community. Being prayerful does not necessarily mean saying many prayers but allowing our prayer to change us and how we relate to others.

The Constitutions recognise that we need to discuss common concerns and so the community meeting is an important element in community life. If we do not discuss things which concern us, they will become problems which can destroy the harmony of any community. The community meeting needs to look at business but also at the spiritual aspects of community life. There are certain basic skills needed to organise and run a successful community meeting. If you know that you do not have them, or suspect this to be the case, try asking one of the other brothers to chair meetings or perhaps the chairing could be shared.

We are also encouraged to share the common table and recreation together. If we never spend time together, we will never grow in unity. If we do spend time together, there is a risk of conflict of course but if good will exists and a willingness to dialogue, then these problems can be overcome and be in fact a bond of unity between us. Each of us must examine our own conscience. Am I truly willing to dialogue with my brothers? Am I always right and the others always wrong? Could some of their criticisms have an element of truth? If so what will I do about it?

Finally we are encouraged to work together and to share our joys, our anxieties and friendships. It is important to celebrate together the ordinary human things like birthdays or anniversaries etc. It is also important to be there for one another when we are in trouble. Always safeguarding the community's right to some privacy, it is very helpful to be able to share our own personal friends with the community.

Religious community is a human reality and therefore is flawed but it is the ambient in which we have been called to respond to God's gratuitous love for us. It is the privileged place where we can grow as human beings, as Christians and as religious. Let us accept one another with all our faults, strive to love one another as Christ has loved us and value one another as brothers and co-heirs of God's Kingdom. Of course we will fail from time to time to live up to our high ideals but that is no reason to let go of these ideals and settle for an unhappy mediocrity. Christ has promised to be with us and we can depend on that promise. If we allow him, he will love our brothers through us. If our experience of community has not been good, why not try to follow the principle of our brother, St. John of the Cross who said, "Where there is no love, put love and you will find love." If there is love within a community, all obstacles can be overcome. Life will not be perfect but we will know that we are accepted for who we are which will give us the confidence to go out to others and share that love with them. Our community lives will bear witness to the truth of the Gospel that Christ has broken down the barriers which separated people from one another and that his love can heal.

If we are willing to take the risk of loving our brothers, we will fulfil the article of our Constitutions which says,

> "Fraternal life modelled on the Jerusalem community is an incarnation of God's gratuitous love, internalised through an ongoing process by which we empty ourselves of all egocentricity - which can affect groups as much as individuals - as we move towards authentic centering in God. In this way we express the charismatic and prophetic nature of the consecrated Carmelite life, weaving harmoniously into it the personal charisms of each member, in the service of the Church and the world." (n. 30).

THE PROPHETIC ELEMENT OF THE CARMELITE CHARISM

Every Christian shares in the threefold dignity of Christ - priest, prophet and king. We Carmelites have had a particular prophetic thrust from the very beginnings of our Order coming from the Elijan aspect of our spirituality. The figure of Elijah the contemplative has had a great impact on our spirituality. From him we learn to listen for the voice of God in the unexpected. God was not in the earthquake or the great fire or the mighty wind but in the sound of a gentle breeze, as it was known for many years, or "in silence" as it is more commonly translated now. The experience of Elijah has given courage to many generations of Carmelites. He believed that he spoke in the name of God and he had won a wonderful victory on Mount Carmel. However he also had to learn how God acts and so when his victory was not followed by even greater success but by serious threats on his life, he became depressed. He went into the desert, sat under a tree and wished he were dead. However God did not allow him to give up. The angel of the Lord, who can come in many different forms, gave him the necessary strength to continue his journey.

When he arrived at Mount Horeb, he had to learn that God's ways are not our ways and God's thoughts are not our thoughts. God asked him, "What are you doing here, Elijah?" (1 Kings 19,9) Elijah answered, "I am zealous with great zeal for the Lord God of hosts …for the Israelites have abandoned your covenant. They have thrown down your altars and have put your prophets to the sword. Only I remain and now they are seeking to kill me." The Lord, after having come to Elijah in the sound of silence, reminded him that that there were at least seven thousand people in Israel who had not bent the knee to Baal or kissed him.

In recent years the Carmelite Family has become aware of the importance of the Prophet Elijah as an inspiration in the work of justice and peace. His contemplative experience impelled him to prophetic action. He denounced without fear the actions of the powerful people of his day and he brought the light of the Word of God into situations of sin. The story of Naboth's vineyard (1 K.21) is a good example of Elijah' s prophetic activity. King Acab wanted Naboth's vineyard for himself but Naboth did not want to sell his patrimony. The Queen, Jezebel, mocked her husband and challenged him to show who in fact was King in Israel. The queen had hatched a diabolical plot to accuse Naboth unjustly of blasphemy and to assume the control of the vineyard when Naboth was out of the way. The Prophet Elijah came on to the scene when Acab had taken the vineyard into his possession and he condemned Acab for abusing his authority. Obviously this was a very courageous step. Proclaiming the Word of God in certain situations can be very dangerous. The stories regarding the Prophet Elijah help us to focus specifically on the prophetic aspect of our vocation. We see a man who translated his contemplative experience into prophetic action and therefore is an excellent model for all Carmelites who are involved in an active apostolate.

To work for justice is an essential element of the preaching of the Gospel. This has been underlined innumerable times in church documents. However those who work in the area of justice and peace often meet with incomprehension or even antagonism from their own brothers or sisters. Why is not easy to explain but this fact has obscured a very important element of our work as religious.

God is not deaf to the cry of the poor and neither must we be deaf. In the words of the Prophet Isaiah, God says, "Is not this rather the fast which I desire: break unjust fetters, untie the thongs of the yoke, set free the oppressed and break every yoke? Does it not consist perhaps in sharing your bread with the hungry and to bring the oppressed and homeless into your own home, in clothing those who are naked without neglecting your own people?" (Is. 58, 6-7). We live in God's world and creation has been entrusted to us as God's stewards. This does not mean that we have complete liberty to use or abuse the goods of the earth without thought for tomorrow or for future generations. We have certain rights but also certain duties towards the rest of creation. The Word of God is concerned with the whole of life and not just spiritual things. Elijah, the man of God, is at the same time a contemplative and also a prophet. Perhaps because he was a contemplative , he was able to be a prophet. Thus Elijah is a model for all Carmelites.

Jesus Christ is for us the primary model of what it means to be a prophet. We are above all followers of Christ and therefore we must seek to put into practice his teachings every day. Jesus Christ is priest, prophet and king because in him all the promises and roles of the Old Testament are fulfilled. He is the one in whom the work of the prophets reaches its culmination. The prophets of the Old Testament proclaimed the Word of God in particular situations. They warned and condemned but also comforted the people in times of difficulty. They sought to turn the hearts of the people towards God and they spoke with severity or with tenderness according to the situation.

Jesus Christ is the Word of God, God's yes to the world. By means of his death and resurrection we are redeemed and reunited with God. The Word of God does not return to Him without having completed what it was sent to do, according to the prophet Isaiah. This is true in a sublime way in the case of Jesus Christ through whom the whole of creation finds once again the road which leads to God. The prophets described the personal relationship which God had with the people as like a marriage. In Christ, God and the human family are united in a way which goes way beyond what the prophets spoke of and they can never be divided.

A prophet is someone who proclaims the Word of God in particular situations. Do not trust a person who wants to be a prophet or who believes himself or herself to be a prophet. A true prophet is one who is sent by God. This mandate gives a certain amount of confidence but also profound humility with the realisation that the choice of God is not based on merit but that God chooses the weak and makes them strong in bearing witness to Him. Pride is the sign of a false prophet.

The Word of God is like a double sided sword which penetrates between the bones and the marrow. Often this is most uncomfortable first of all for the prophet but always for those who listen.

Some people are called to be prophets like those of the Old Testament but I think that this is a rare vocation. Nevertheless we are all called by means of our Christian and Carmelite vocation to share in the prophetic function of Christ, bringing the Word of God into every situation in which we find ourselves. This does not mean finding an explicit Biblical text for the situation but it means to give God the space to shape our hearts according to His Word so that our very presence becomes a word from God.

All of this is easy to say but how do we accomplish it in practice? We accepted Christ's call to follow him with the best of intentions. We had high ideals and generosity. Over time perhaps the experience of life has changed our ideals somewhat but hopefully has not destroyed them. Fundamentally the mission of all Christians is the same - to continue the presence and work of Jesus Christ in our world. The way we do this can and must change as circumstances change. No individual and no religious group can on its own fully reflect or fully represent the fullness of Christ and therefore every religious family has its particular charism which represents one aspect of the work of Christ. We cannot change our charism which is the gift of God to us for the world. Our charism defines the form of our participation in the mission of the Church. Mission and charism are intimately linked.

An essential element of the Carmelite charism is the contemplative aspect which has an intimate connection with the prophetic dimension. By responding to the challenge of the contemplative dimension of our vocation we become a word from God to our society which is the fundamental mission of a prophet.

To become a word from God it is necessary to enter a process of interior transformation and consent to the presence and action of God in our life. This is the work of God but God will not do it without our consent. This process can be painful because through it we come to see ourselves as we really are and not as we would like to be. The great danger is that we will seek to run away from this encounter with ourselves because we do not want to accept what is being revealed to us. This process of transformation includes a disintegration of what is false within us so that the true self can come to birth.

The false self is a defence which each one of us constructs around ourselves against a perceived danger, that is a threat to our need for esteem, our instinct for survival and our need to control our environment. If we think that these basic human needs are not being satisfied, and they never will be satisfied because they are insatiable, they can never have enough of a good thing, then we will seek to satisfy them in whatever way is open to us. We will seek esteem and affection from our families and friends, from the members of our community, from our superiors, from the people we serve in our apostolic work. We will seek signs of security everywhere. We will seek to have control over our own lives and also the lives of those people who enter our sphere of influence.

The false self is very subtle and can find a whole host of reasons for not changing. It is even more subtle when it manages to convince us that it does not exist. The false self is perfectly content in whatever way of life it happens to find itself. It can wear a religious habit - it does not matter - it simply changes its way of working. In the Gospel when Jesus says that one must lose one's life in order to find it, it is the false self which must die in order to discover the true self which is created in the image of God. However we do not want to lose this false self because it is the only self we know. For this reason the spiritual journey, which is simple is at the same time very difficult.

We do not fulfil our prophetic vocation simply by preaching or when we work with the poor and the emarginated, vital though that work is. We fulfil our prophetic vocation when we become a word from God and this involves a death in view of a resurrection, a new life in the image of God.

The prophets of the Old Testament spoke to the imagination. They asked the people to imagine another possible future. For example the prophets Isaiah and Mica spoke in a time of war of a time of peace when "from their swords they will forge ploughshares and from their blades, scythes. No nation will lift the sword against another nation and they will not learn the art of war anymore..." When the future is very dark, the prophets bring hope. However in order to do this, it is necessary to see beyond the present situation to the reality which lies beneath. This is the faith of Our Lady in the

Magnificat who sees the proud cast down, the hungry filled with good things and the rich sent away empty when those who see only the external appearances would believe the opposite to be true.

Carmel is famous for its marian devotion which is expressed in many ways. The greatest devotion is to be conformed to the object of our devotion. Titus Brandsma said that the vocation of a Carmelite was to be another Mary. The "yes" of Mary gave the necessary space for Christ to be born. Through her, God now has a human face. Our devotion to Mary must not stop at the imitation of her virtues, though that is very important. We must allow Christ to grow within us so that we become transformed in him so that we can say with St. Paul, "it is no longer I who live but Christ who lives in me". (Gal. 2,20) In that way we will be a word from God, a tabernacle of the presence of God in the world. In that way we will live our prophetic vocation.

I believe that St. Thérèse of Lisieux was a prophet sent by God to remind the world of the simplicity of the Good News when it was obscured by human ideas of holiness. In the time of Thérèse, there was great emphasis on moral perfection and purity as a condition of approaching God. Thus the spiritual life was hard and rather grim. Thérèse was aware that she was not able to climb the huge mountains of spiritual perfection, but did not become discouraged but entrusted herself to the Merciful Love of God who raises little ones to the top of the mountain.

Abandoning ourselves into the hands of God with the desire of being whatever God wants us to be, disposes us completely to the action of God. Then we will be a word from God in every situation in which we find ourselves. This might mean that we are called upon to do something very important or perhaps we will be forgotten by everyone. Remember the example used by Thérèse of the different types of flowers all of which give pleasure to God. Some flowers are bigger or brighter than others or with a more beautiful perfume but God takes pleasure in all of them.

Fulfilling our prophetic vocation as members of the Carmelite family is a great challenge for each of us but it is not something which we can do with our own strength. We will be faithful to our vocation inasmuch as we consent to the purifying and transforming action of God in our lives. God will shape us and form us to become a word from Him. In this process Our Lady is the greatest example we have.

As St. Thérèse said,

"Holiness does not consist in this or that practice. It consists in a disposition of heart which makes us humble and small in the arms of God, aware of our own weakness and daringly confident in His Fatherly goodness." (NV)

THE SPIRITUAL JOURNEY

As we prepare to celebrate the new millennium we experience ourselves as part of a world which is full of contradictions. Our world is plagued by wars, famine, hatred and yet at the same time people of faith can see signs of hope, sometimes only little seeds, but these signs give us hope and the strength to continue to work in the face of what can often seem to be impossible odds.

We are privileged to live at one of those rare and most exciting times in history when there is a profound cultural shift. It was said during the General Chapter 1995 that God is purifying the Church and bringing it back to the purity of its origins. There are many double-sided events in our day. On the one hand, we lament the lack of vocations, the decreasing numbers of people coming to church, the increasing secularisation of society. On the other hand we can see in these same events the hand of God at work. As was stated in the final document of the General Chapter, now is not a time for pessimism. The signs of the times announce the coming of a new springtime for Christianity.

Given the present situation, what should be our response? The Church has asked all Christians to co-operate in an era of new evangelisation. The Church is missionary by its very nature and so must our Order be. Let us remain open to the promptings of the Spirit and continue to read the signs of the times and respond in the future as we have done in the past.

There are many ways to respond to the needs of the world and the call of Christ to preach the Gospel to all nations. Our way is the Carmelite way. It is not better or worse than any other way but it is our way. The best way for us to respond to the Church's call for a new evangelisation is to be what we are intended to be - Carmelites. We may need to change our outlook and our methods but we need not attempt to change what we are.

What are we? What is this Carmelite way? Thankfully to help us answer this question we have the benefit of our new Constitutions which describe our life and mission. We describe ourselves as living in "obsequium Jesu Christi" embracing the Gospel as the supreme norm of our lives co-operating in the realisation of God's plan in our world. (art. 2). We are the Brothers of The Blessed Virgin Mary of Mount Carmel (art. 6) and we are the inheritors of a long tradition.. After many years of discussion and scholarship, I would suggest that who we are is now clear, that is, our charism is clear. We live our following of Christ by committing ourselves to the search for the face of the living God (the contemplative dimension of the Gospel), to fraternity and to service in the midst of the people (art. 14). The experience of the desert is the dynamic unifying factor of these values (art. 15). The Prophet Elijah and Our Lady are especially inspirational to us (art. 25 ff).

One of the main issues facing us in our day is not, "Who are we?" or "What is our place in the Church?" but "How do we live this charism concretely in order to respond to the call of the Church for an era of new evangelisation?" We are told in art. 64 that prayer is the irremoveable centre of our lives and it is from this centre that authentic community and ministry arise. Art. 78 points out that we must be so profoundly contemplative that we see everything that happens almost as if we were looking through God's eyes. We cannot get away from the fact that contemplation is an essential element of our vocation and indeed is the source of our fraternal and apostolic lives. However the term "contemplation" is a difficult one for us and for many Christians for a number of reasons. I think that still many people, Carmelites included, would reject the word as having anything to do with them. They are quite happy to leave that sort of thing to enclosed nuns who are often called "contemplatives". They do not see how contemplation could possibly fit in with their busy lifestyles. Our mendicant status means that we are called to the active apostolate and we know how busy we can be. The opposite reaction is to apply the term "contemplation" to ourselves too easily and therefore domesticate it and reduce it to the banal. We can talk about having a contemplative attitude and practising contemplative prayer without understanding what this means in practice nor accepting what contemplation demands of us.

The way that spirituality has often been presented has hindered many of us from accepting the invitation of God to intimacy. The ascent of Mount Carmel and the dark nights of St. John of the Cross may sound good in spiritual talks but what about their reality? Is it not better just to get on with our pastoral work and leave all that stuff to those who are attracted to it?

In 1997 we celebrated the centenary of the death of St. Therese of Lisieux. Hers was a prophetic voice at a time when the icy hands of Jansenism still maintained a grip on many Christians. She proclaimed once again the Good News of Jesus Christ, that God is love and that we are desired by God who wishes to enter into an intimate relationship of friendship with us. As we quoted in the final document of the General Chapter, "There is no need to be afraid little flock. It is your Father's good pleasure to give you the Kingdom." (Lk. 12,32)

Art. 17 of the Constitutions tells us that contemplation begins when we entrust ourselves to God, *whatever way God chooses to come to us*. It is critical to get a good start on our journey. Obviously we who preach the Gospel are not afraid of God because we preach a God of love but I invite you to look into your heart and see whether you really believe that. If so, then following the example of St. Therese, abandoning yourself into the hands of God will be a simple matter. Faith of course is not just a matter of feelings and so it is not necessary to feel trust in order to truly entrust ourselves to God. However we need to stay awake and recognise the approach of God who may come to us in totally unexpected ways. Mary received the Word of God through the message of an angel but was also open to hearing God's voice at the foot of the cross. Elijah met God not in the earthquake or the fire or the mighty wind but in the sound of a gentle breeze. I would suggest that one of the most unexpected ways that God chooses to come to us is through our brother with whom we live in community.

Art. 17 goes on to tell us that contemplation is an attitude of openness to God whose presence we discover everywhere. Our preaching or teaching or whatever work we do does not bring Christ to people but hopefully helps them to discover His presence in their lives or be more aware of it. Christ is already present in each situation and individual before we arrive. Above all our daily lives, our presence, should reveal something of God. Does it? Can we really discover the presence of God everywhere even in difficulties? This is the faith of Our Lady in the Magnificat who praises God for throwing down the proud, feeding the hungry and sending the rich away empty when most people would see the opposite as true. A contemplative is able to see beyond the externals to the reality beneath. A constant attitude of openness to God is of course not easy because the presence of God calls into question how we live and constantly calls us to conversion which means change and we are not always very keen to change.

Contemplation, according to the same article of the Constitutions, constitutes the interior journey of the Carmelite which begins with the completely free initiative of God who touches us and transforms us towards a unity of love with Him, raising us up to be able to freely enjoy being loved by God and living in His loving presence. Now please notice that the article does not discriminate; it does not say that this is reserved for some Carmelites - for the holy ones, or for enclosed nuns; it just says "the Carmelite" , that is all who are called to Carmel are called to this. Contemplation is not for an elite; it is for everyone; it is for you and I. Contemplation has little if anything to do with strange phenomena; it has everything to do with entrusting ourselves to God and allowing God to love us into true life. Contemplation is not a reward for virtue but is what makes us able to be virtuous. It is the space for God to transform us from within so that as article 17 says, our human, limited and imperfect ways of thinking, loving and acting are emptied and transformed into divine ways.

But what is wrong with our human ways of thinking, loving and acting? They are limited and imperfect and because of this they are often distorted and manipulated by motives of which we are totally unaware or barely aware. Article 18 of the Constitutions tells us that contemplation is not only the source of our spiritual life but *determines* the quality of our fraternal life and of our service in the midst of the people. Without contemplation, without entering this process whereby God transforms our human, limited and imperfect ways of thinking, loving and acting into divine ways, our community life and ministry will tend to be distorted and manipulative. We must of course work on the quality of our community lives and our ministry but without the openness to God and the willingness to change, our efforts will not have much effect although God can raise up children from stones and so uses our limited and imperfect ways to perform wonders.

In the 60's there was a debate within the Order about how to balance the contemplative and active elements of our vocation and indeed Carmelites have always lived with this tension. There was a suggestion that it was very unfair to Carmelites working in busy parishes or schools to say that the principal part of our vocation is contemplation as was said in the Constitutions of that time. I believe that this issue emerged from a wrong understanding of contemplation. It was thought for hundreds of years that contemplation was for an elite group and certainly not for everyone and so most Carmelites felt themselves to be excluded from this and gave themselves very generously to their apostolic work and left contemplation to others. Therefore it really was a problem for them to read in the Constitutions of the time that contemplation was the principal part of their vocation. In our day we are witnessing an upsurge of interest in contemplation among religious but especially among lay people. People are searching for more; they are searching for depth; they are searching for something which will respond to their deeply-felt hunger; they are searching for God. If we pat them on the head and tell them not to worry about things like that, they will go away and never come back. They will seek an answer elsewhere.

If contemplation is really for everyone and is not reserved for enclosed nuns and monks or those with a great deal of leisure time, it must be possible in the midst of a busy apostolic ministry. Indeed if we are to believe our Constitutions, contemplation will actually determine the quality of our ministry and our community life. It is of course all very well talking about the glories of contemplation or the need for it but what can we do about it practically in the midst of our busy lives? The first and most important thing to remember is that contemplation is God's work and God's gift which is freely given whenever and to whomever God wishes. Responding to the grace of God, we entrust ourselves into the arms of God who loves us - we may not necessarily feel this but we believe it. We can prepare the way for the Lord like John the Baptist by examining our lives and see-ing if there is anything which is incompatible with our vocation. We can then use the normal remedies which we are offered through the Church. However perhaps we are not ready to change or perhaps there are some elements of our character which we cannot change at present. That need not hold us back . God is far greater than our weaknesses and God's mercy is more powerful than our sins and defects.

We are told in art. 80 of the Constitutions that silent prayer is of very great help in increasing the spirit of contemplation and that we must dedicate an adequate time each day to it. What is an adequate time? You alone can answer that in the circumstances of your own life but remember if we are too busy to pray, then we are too busy. We are encouraged elsewhere to practice Lectio Divina which is becoming a great force within our Order. Of course Lectio and silent prayer can be combined very easily. The traditional practice of Lectio gives space for Lectio, Meditatio and Oratio where we read the Word of God, reflect on it and respond to it in prayer. There is of course a fourth step - contemplatio. Reading, reflecting and respond-ing are all good but of course they utilise the human, limited and imperfect ways of thinking and loving. The stage of contemplatio is where we let go of these limited ways for a short period and allow God to act.in us. So we are invited to simply rest in God beyond words, beyond thoughts, beyond our activity and leave the rest to God. When or if this silence becomes contemplation is best left in God's hands. However in the silence we slowly learn a new language which transcends our poor limited human words and then silence becomes far more eloquent than many words.

What happens when we let go of our pious words and thoughts? We find ourselves thinking of what is for lunch or planning our next homily or having an internal argument with someone who has wronged us in the past. When we become aware of this, we may very well feel that this silent prayer business is not for us, that we cannot do it and that we had better stick to meditation where we have something to occupy our busy minds. I suggest that this reac-tion, while understandable, is mistaken. What really matters in our prayer is not our words or thoughts, important though these are, but our *desire*. What do you really desire? As you know it is very possible for the lips to say one thing and for the heart to say the opposite. God reads the heart; God knows the desire of our heart even though our minds may seem to be far away. Obviously when we become aware that we are distracted, we can choose to continue thinking about our next homily or whatever but that would be changing our intention to simply be in God's presence. It is better just to renew our intention to be in God's presence and to be open to God's action and we can do so in many ways, for example by the use of a simple word or even an interior glance towards God. It may be that the use of many words or even holy thoughts is not helpful at this time. We have all had the experience in a human relationship where silence speaks far more eloquently than many words. Even very busy people can maintain intimate human relationships and so in the midst of our busy lives we are invited into an intimate relationship with God. Indeed with this relationship at the centre of our lives, all our activity and our community lives will become much more fruitful.

If we accept God's invitation to begin this interior journey, we will of course meet with difficulties on the way because we will be brought face to face with ourselves. We will see ever more clearly the motives for our actions. We will see that sometimes even our best actions have selfish motives. This is very difficult to accept and this is why the spiritual journey is so difficult and why many would seem to turn back to a less challenging place. If however we but knew the gift God was offering us, we would continue our journey despite the painful revelations about ourselves which we were offered. On this journey we become less proud, less sure of our own virtue but more reliant on the mercy of God and more aware that all human beings are our brothers and sisters.

I believe that we will respond to the call of the Pope for an era of new evangelisation and be people of the new millennium insofar as we are faithful to our vocation which is described in our Constitutions. If we take seriously the contemplative aspect of our vocation, the other aspects will also become much more fruitful. Our community lives will become much more human because as we become more aware we will more easily accept the failings of our brothers. Our apostolic work will become much more fruitful, which is not the same as being successful. We will become even more missionary because as our Constitutions tell us, "our human ways of thinking, loving and acting will be changed into divine ways" (art. 17). We will see reality as if through the eyes of God and love the whole of reality as if with the heart of God.

Our world is undergoing great cultural upheaval as we approach the new millennium. There is a profound spiritual crisis in our times. What have we to say in this situation? What can we do with this great opportunity? We can of course do whatever our skills permit us to do but above all we can all re-commit ourselves daily to the vocation to which we have been called. Simply by living as Carmelites, we will speak a powerful word to our world because it will be a word from God.

THE PRAYER OF SILENCE

In the Rule of St. Albert can be found the precept that the hermits on Mount Carmel are to build a chapel in the middle of their cells. This chapel was placed under the protection of Mary, the Lady of the Place, and with this act, the hermits placed their whole lives and the future of their movement under her protection. This simple fact is the beginning of Carmelite Marian devotion.

In the course of the following centuries, the Carmelites underlined various aspects of their relationship with Our Lady. She is Patroness, Mother and Sister. Our Carmelite writers emphasised particular Marian feasts like the Immaculate Conception and the Assumption. Carmelite Marian devotion is not simply a way to admire Our Lady but above all to place her before the eyes of Carmelites as a model for our way of life. The most authentic devotion is to imitate the one to whom we are devoted. The Carmelites of the past saw in Mary the human being who had the most intimate experience of God. The goal of the Carmelite life, according to the 14th century Book of the First Monks, was to offer to God a heart free from the stain of actual sin and to taste even in this life that which pertains to the life to come. This intimate relationship with God by its very nature must overflow in works of love.

Mary listened to the Word of God and received it in her womb. If we want to have a real devotion to Our Lady of Mount Carmel, we must also listen to the Word and welcome it into our lives. The Word will change us radically.

The process whereby we are changed and transformed is called contemplation, which is a central concept of Carmelite spirituality. Contemplation is not a series a particular experiences but a process whereby little by little we are transformed in God. Our destiny is to become like God because we live with the same life as God, that is to say, the Holy Spirit.

Mary is the mother of the divine life in us and as our sister, she accompanies us on our journey. She is our model. However, we already know all this. We have heard it often. We know that we must imitate the virtues of Mary but how? How can we become docile to the will of God, patient, humble and so on?

To become like the Mother of God, to leave space in our lives so that God can grow in us, is the work of God. Certainly we can and must co-operate but the result of this process of transformation remains always God's work.

In what consists our co-operation? Of course we must try to live good Christian lives according to the Gospel. However those who have decided to live according to the Gospel know that this is much easier to say than to do. In the Magnificat, Mary praised and thanked God for having accomplished great things in her. God can also do great things in us if we give God the time and space to work in us, and, above all, if we consent to God's presence and action in our lives.

Lectio Divina is the most traditional way to grow in an intimate relationship with God and it is by means of this relationship that we are transformed and rendered capable of living the Gospel in all its fullness. A monk in the 12th century described the fundamental elements of Lectio Divina:- read the Word of God (lectio); reflect on the Word (meditatio), respond to the Word from the heart (oratio); rest in the Word (contemplatio).

The process of contemplation changes the human ways of thinking, loving and acting into divine ways. Our human ways are very limited and so when we read the Word of God, we are limited by our experience of life and by many other factors. It is said that one can find in the Bible reasons to support any position. It is therefore not sufficient just to read the Bible; our way of looking at things must be purified. When we meditate on the Word of God, we try to understand its meaning and what message it may have for our lives but when we do this, we are still limited. Our little world must be enlarged and our minds reformed according to the mind of Christ. When we pray from the heart, we are still using human words. Our words and thoughts, no matter how beautiful, are still human words and thoughts and it is therefore necessary that they too be purified by the Word of God.

St. John of the Cross wrote that God spoke one word and that word was His Son; this Word God repeats in an eternal silence and in silence must it ever be heard by the soul. Lectio Divina moves towards silence. When our words and our beautiful thoughts are no longer sufficient, only silence can give an adequate response to the Word of God.

Mary was blessed not because she was the physical mother of Jesus but because she heard the Word of God and put it into practice. Mary is our model as to how we can listen to this Word and put it into practice in our own lives.

In order to listen seriously to the Word of God, our receptive faculties must be enlarged and purified. We can and must do our best but in the end only God can bring our work to completion. Our capacity for listening is limited by the filter which each of us has within us. This filter is formed by our motives; some of these we are not even aware of. For example, if I do not believe that I have any need for repentance, I will not hear the appeal of the Gospel to conversion. At least this appeal will not penetrate into my inmost being and therefore no transformation will take place in my life. I am not thinking about a first conversion from a life far from God, but rather I am referring to a second phase of conversion in which we abandon ourselves into the hands of God so that God can accomplish His work in us. St. John of the Cross and St. Teresa of Avila both write of a stage on the spiritual journey which is good but at the same time dangerous. John describes the state of beginners who believe themselves to be much better than they in fact are. St. Teresa, in the Interior Castle, places these people in the 3rd mansions describing them as good Christians but whose lives are guided by good sense and who still lack an ardent love and who must be transformed in God.

The process of transformation normally takes place in and through all the events of daily life. The first part of this process of transformation is called by John of the Cross, the night of sense which is only the beginning. The real purification and transformation takes place in the second part of the night, the darkest part but closer to the dawn. The dark night is a blessing because it is an effect of the process of contemplation which is an inflow of God into the soul. God is light but the light is so brilliant that it appears to be darkness to the human being.

God speaks to us in the silence of the night. In concrete terms what actually happens when we experience silence? Often we feel rather uncomfortable because we are not used to silence. Our world is filled with noise – radio, television, constant chatting about this and that – words, words, words. When we pray, we do not change our human nature and so for this reason we may find silence difficult even at times of prayer. There exists the temptation even to fill the entire experience of Lectio Divina with words. Of course it is necessary to take time to read the Word of God, to meditate on it and to pray it with words and thoughts which arise spontaneously from our hearts but it is equally important to leave space for silence where God speaks to us in the sound of a gentle breeze.

The voice of God is so gentle that we run the risk of suffocating it with the noise within ourselves. Consciously we enter into silence and leaving aside our beautiful words and holy thoughts for a moment, we reserve a space which we hope God will fill. I have often been surprised by the number of people who do not seem to understand the value of silence and who cannot appreciate its place in Christian prayer.

The silence to which I am referring is not merely an empty space, a lack of words; it is a desire to which God alone can respond. There is a type of silence which is not Christian. Everything depends on one's intention. If we want to use the time of silence to sleep or daydream or for relaxation, that is not Christian prayer. It is, however, possible to enter into silence with the best of intentions and after a few minutes to fall asleep or become distracted but if our intention is to communicate with God, Father, Son and Holy Spirit, it remains prayer. To appreciate the value of silence, we must be convinced that God lives and works in us whether we are awake or asleep. God does not need our beautiful words and holy thoughts but our desire. What do we really desire? If we really desire that God transform us, He will do it. However it is possible to use words and thoughts in order to stay just as we are but to feel that we are really making headway on the spiritual journey.

I would like to propose a method of prayer which can make silence very fruitful. It is a method of Christian prayer based on the very rich Christian contemplative tradition and especially on a classic book from this tradition, "The Cloud of Unknowing", written by an unknown author in the 15th century. If one is praying at all, one is using some method of prayer, whether from a traditional source or from one's own ingenuity. The method which I am proposing is not intended to replace whatever method one is using but it can make other ways of prayer more fruitful. This method has helped me greatly and I simply want to share it. The most important thing for this method of prayer is to be convinced that God is not far away but in fact is very near. God has set up home in our hearts.

This method of prayer can be called the prayer of silence or the prayer of desire but it is most often called centering prayer[1]. In the silence we tend towards God with our desire. First of all try to find a place where interruptions will be reduced to a minimum, then get yourself into a comfortable position which you can maintain for the whole period of prayer. A minimum of twenty minutes is recommended. To set the mood, one could begin by reading a small portion of Scripture. We do not want to think of the meaning of these words; meditation is for another time. We desire only to be in the presence of God and to consent to God's action. This is not a prayer of attention but intention.

After having settled down and set the mood, the next step of this simple way of prayer is to close one's eyes and silently introduce a sacred word into one's consciousness. A sacred word is a word which has great significance for you in your relationship with God but it need not be a traditionally "holy" word. Take the example of the little word "yes". It can mean very little or a great deal depending on the circumstances and the intention of the person speaking. Also in a very close relationship, a couple may have pet names for each other, These names may be very meaningful within the relationship but they could sound very silly to a third party. The word which you choose should be sacred for you. According to the teaching of the 'Cloud of Unknowing", it is better if the word you choose be brief, one syllable if possible. I can suggest some possible words:- "God, Lord, Abba, Father, Spirit, Jesus, Mary, Yes, Peace, Love, Joy".

When I say, introduce the sacred word into one's consciousness, I do not mean to pronounce the word aloud or even silently in one's mind but to welcome the word within oneself without pondering on its meaning. It is not necessary to use great mental force with this word; it is introduced very, very gently. The sacred word is not a mantra; it is not repeated continually during the prayer but is used only when necessary, when we find that we are thinking of something instead of simply being in the presence of God and consenting to God's action. The sacred word focuses our desire and we use the word always in the same way to return our heart to the Lord when we become aware that we are thinking of something. Our intention is simply to be in the presence of God and consent to God's action in our lives. Our sacred word expresses our intention and so when we become aware that we are thinking of something, we can decide either to continue thinking about whatever we became aware of or to return to our original intention of simply being in God's presence and consenting to God's action. This we do by re-introducing ever so gently the sacred word which we have chosen.

During the period of this prayer, it is not the time to speak to God in words or have holy thoughts. We can do all this at another time. Our silence and our desire are worth much more than many words.

By means of the sacred word which we have chosen, we express our desire and our intention to remain in the presence of God and to consent to God's purifying and transforming action. We return to the sacred word, which is the symbol of our intention and desire, only when we are aware that we are thinking about something. There is no point in getting upset at our distractions but we return very gently to our sacred word as the symbol of our intention to remain in God's presence and to submit to and co-operate with God's action in our lives. The prayer itself consists simply in being in the presence of God without thinking of anything in particular. It is a prayer of relationship with God, Father, Son and Holy Spirit. If we understand how to be with another person in silence without thinking of anything or doing anything, then we can understand this prayer. This method of prayer can be helpful to those who feel within themselves a call to silence.

Practical guidelines for Centering Prayer

There are four simple guidelines to the method of Centering Prayer. These are:-

1. *Choose a Sacred Word as the symbol of your intention to consent to the presence and action of God within.*

2. *Sitting comfortably and with eyes closed, settle briefly and silently introduce the Sacred Word as the symbol of your intention to consent to God's presence and action.*

3. *When you become aware of thoughts return ever so gently to the Sacred Word*

4. *At the end of the prayer period, remain in silence for a few minutes with eyes closed.*

[1] Centering Prayer was taught originally by three Trappist monks in the USA who had made a profound study of the Christian Contemplative Tradition. The basic book to learn more about this way of prayer is by Thomas Keating OCSO, *Open Mind, Open Heart. The Contemplative Dimension of the Gospel,* Element Books, Mass., USA, 1992